TREES LETTERS

by Arimi

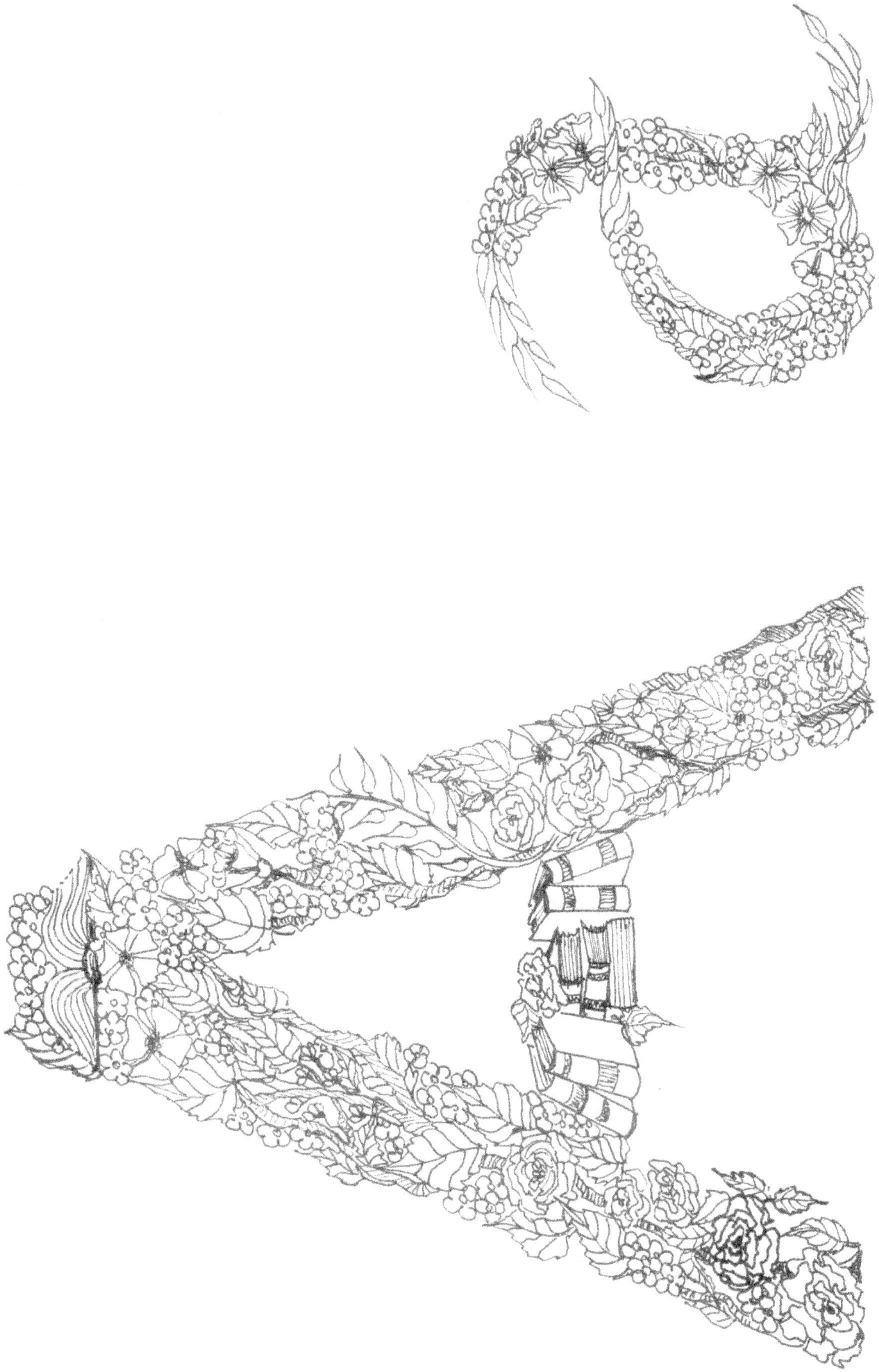

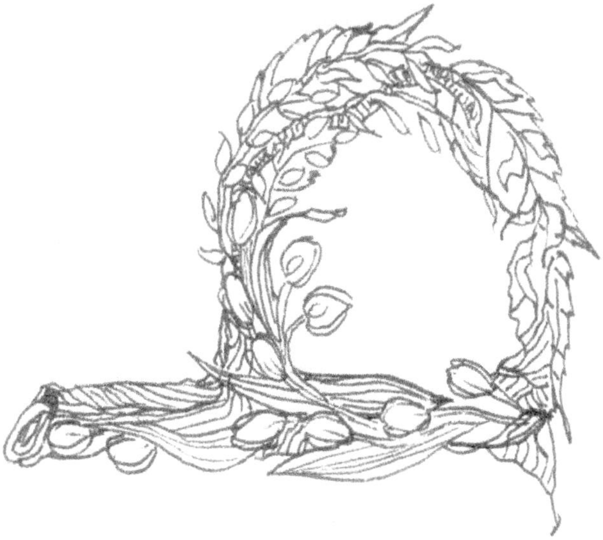

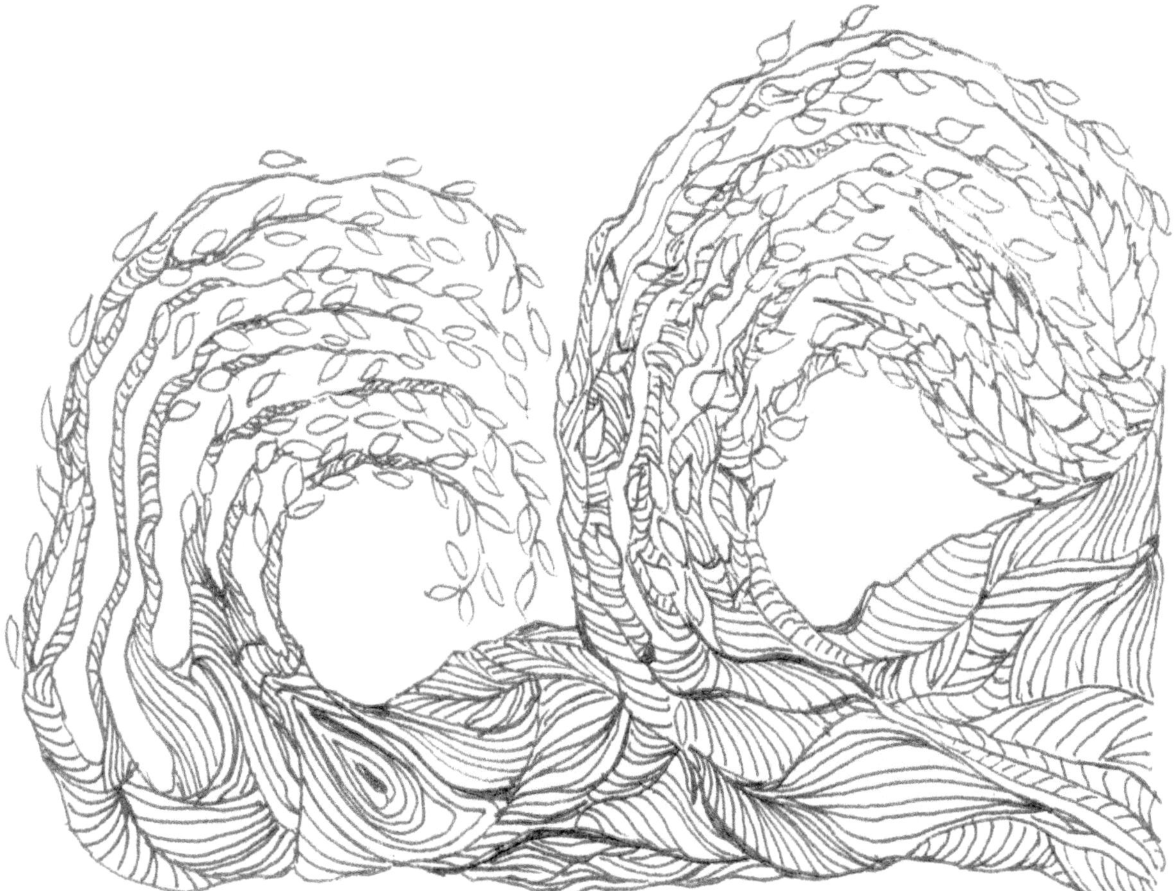

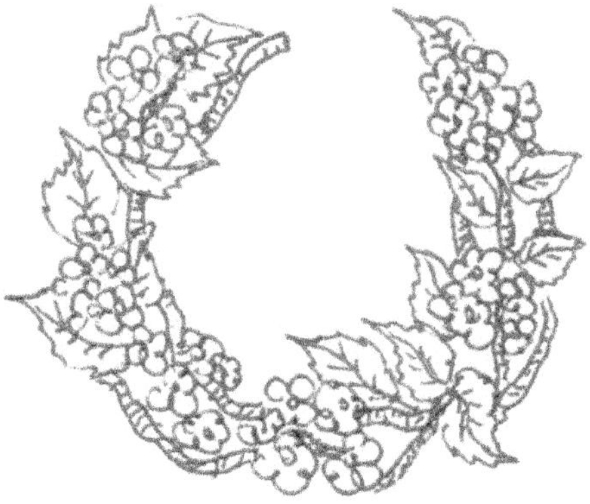
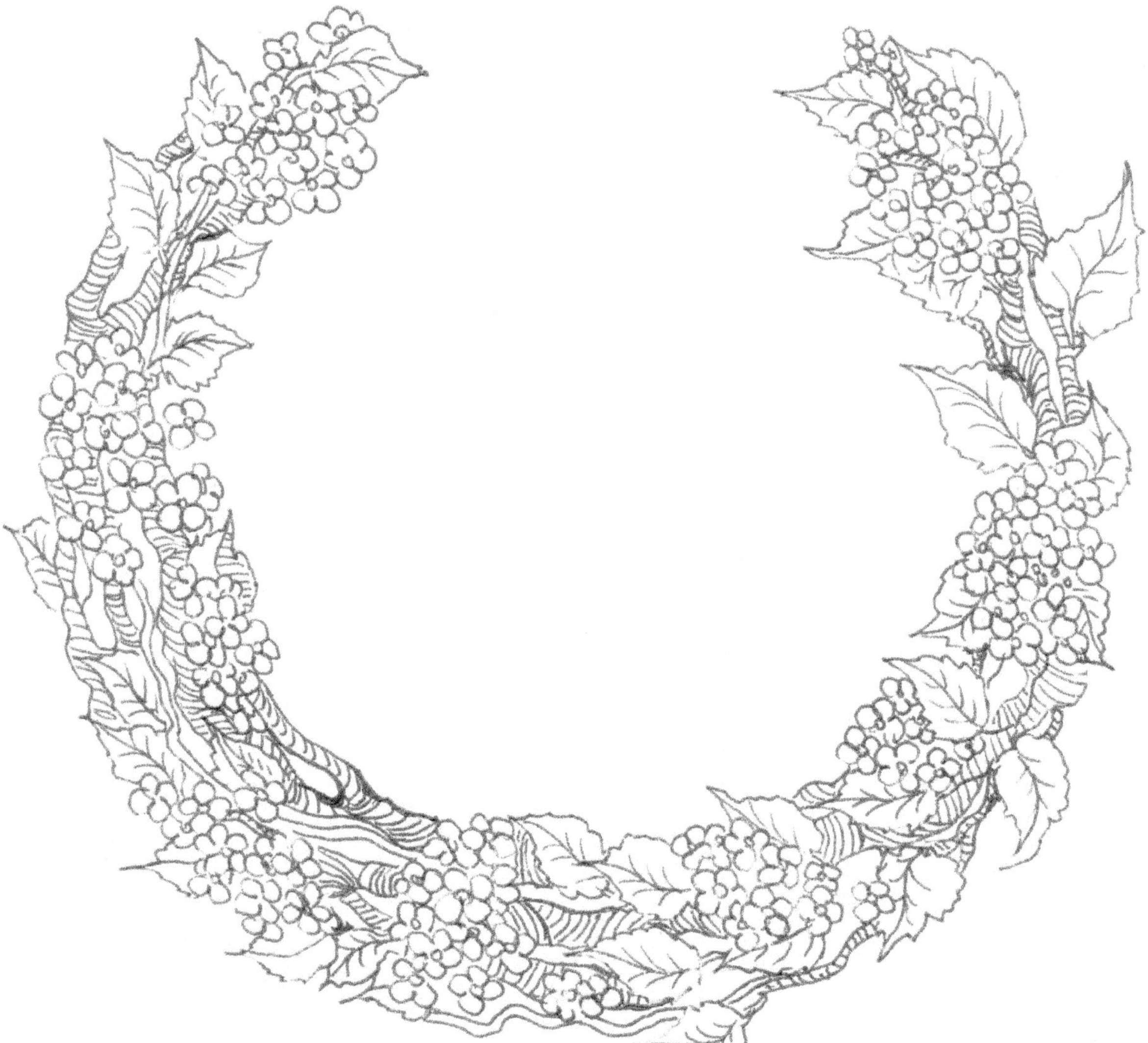

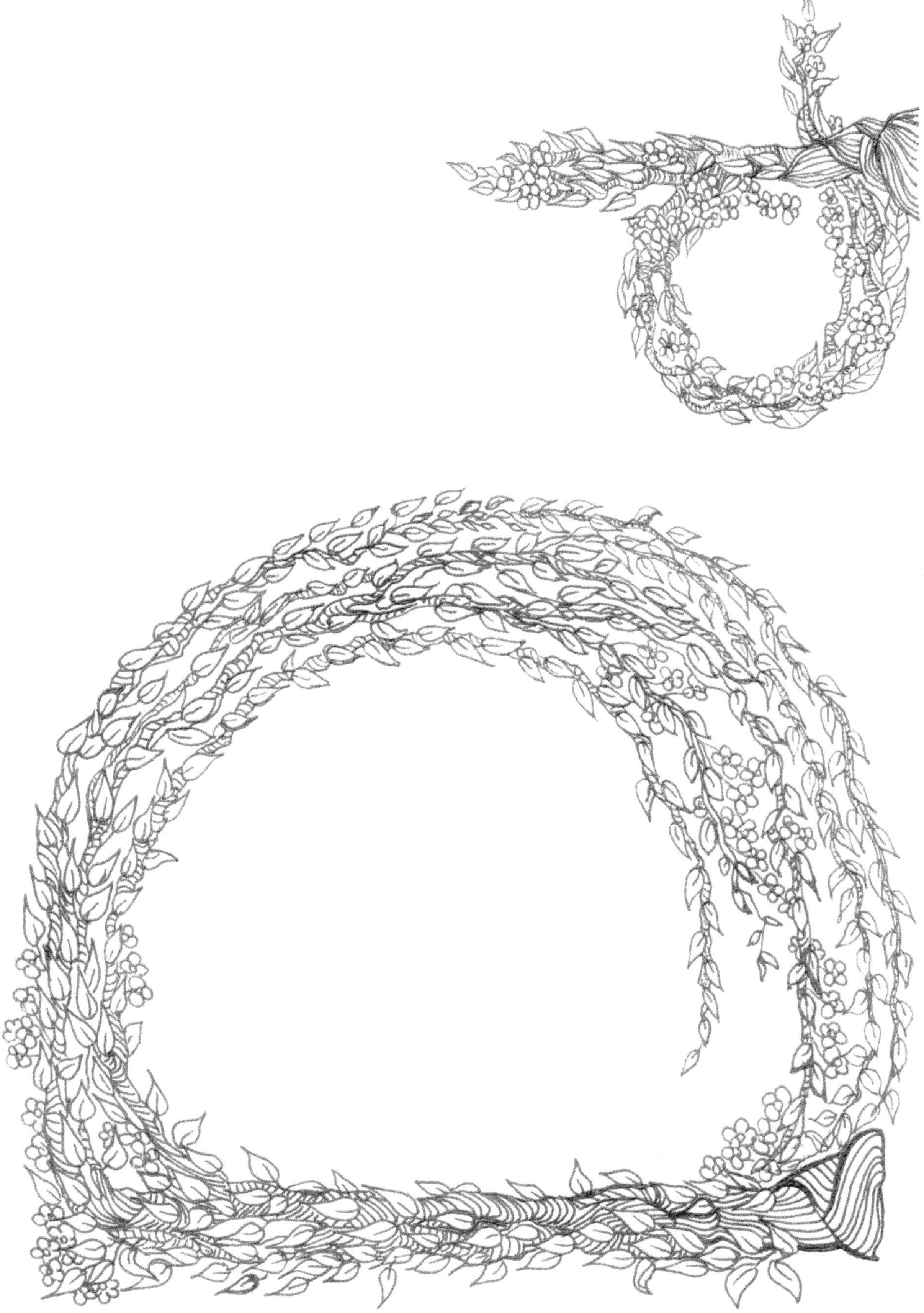

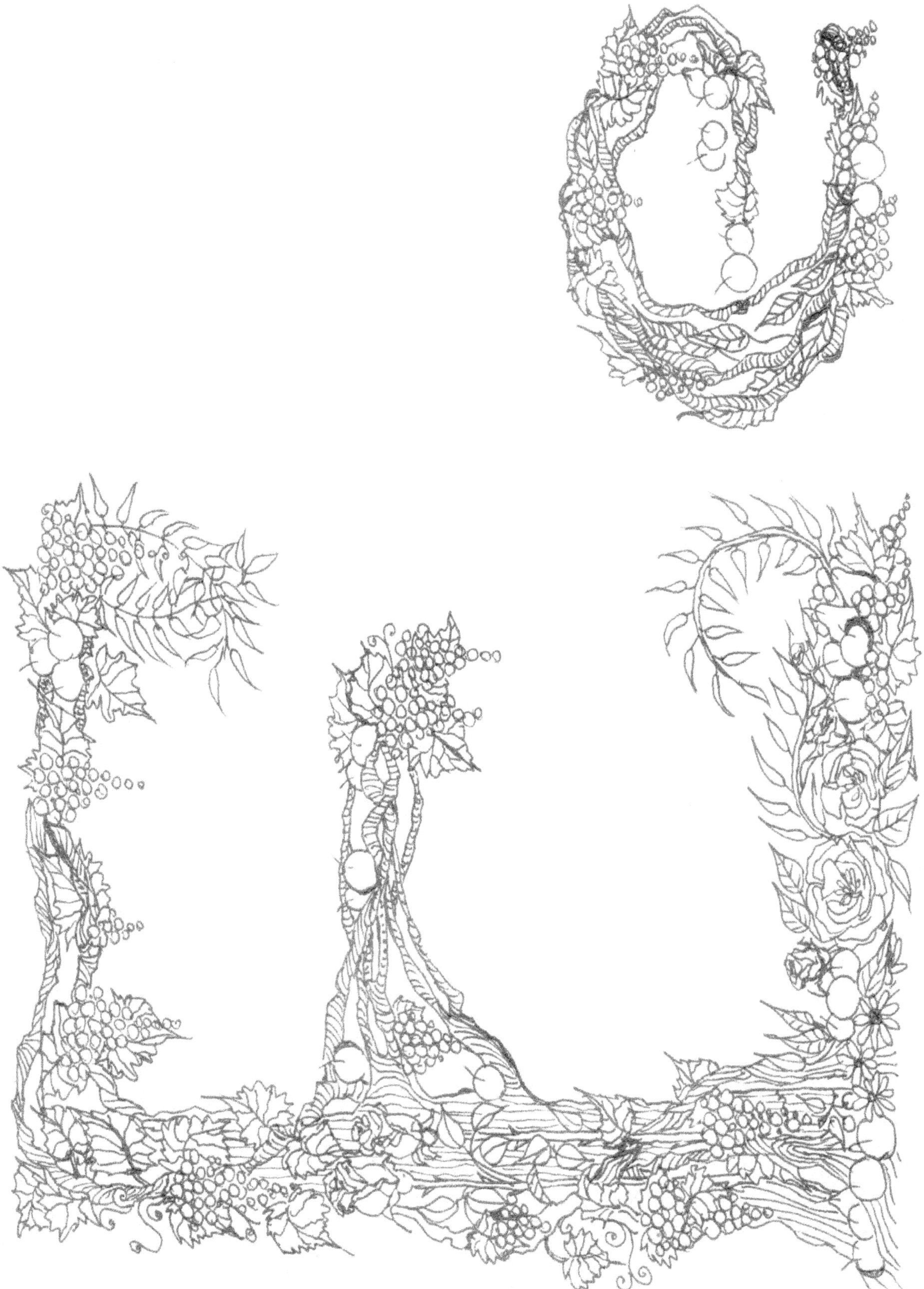

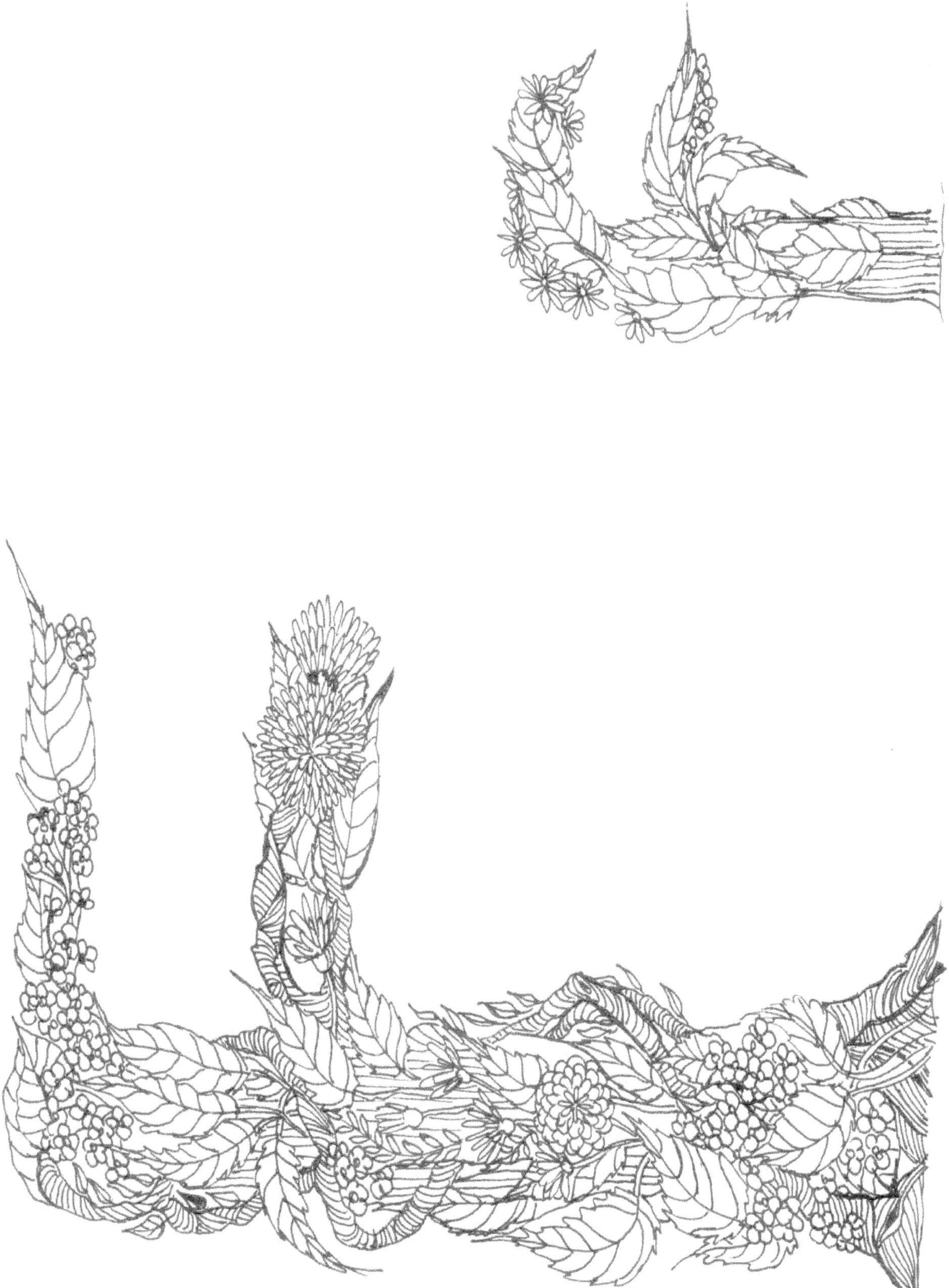

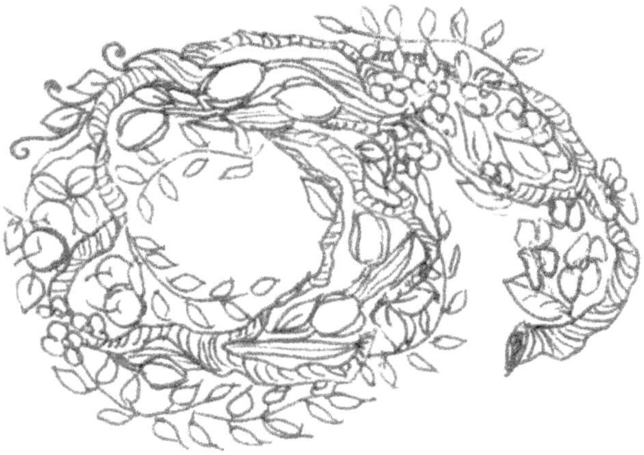

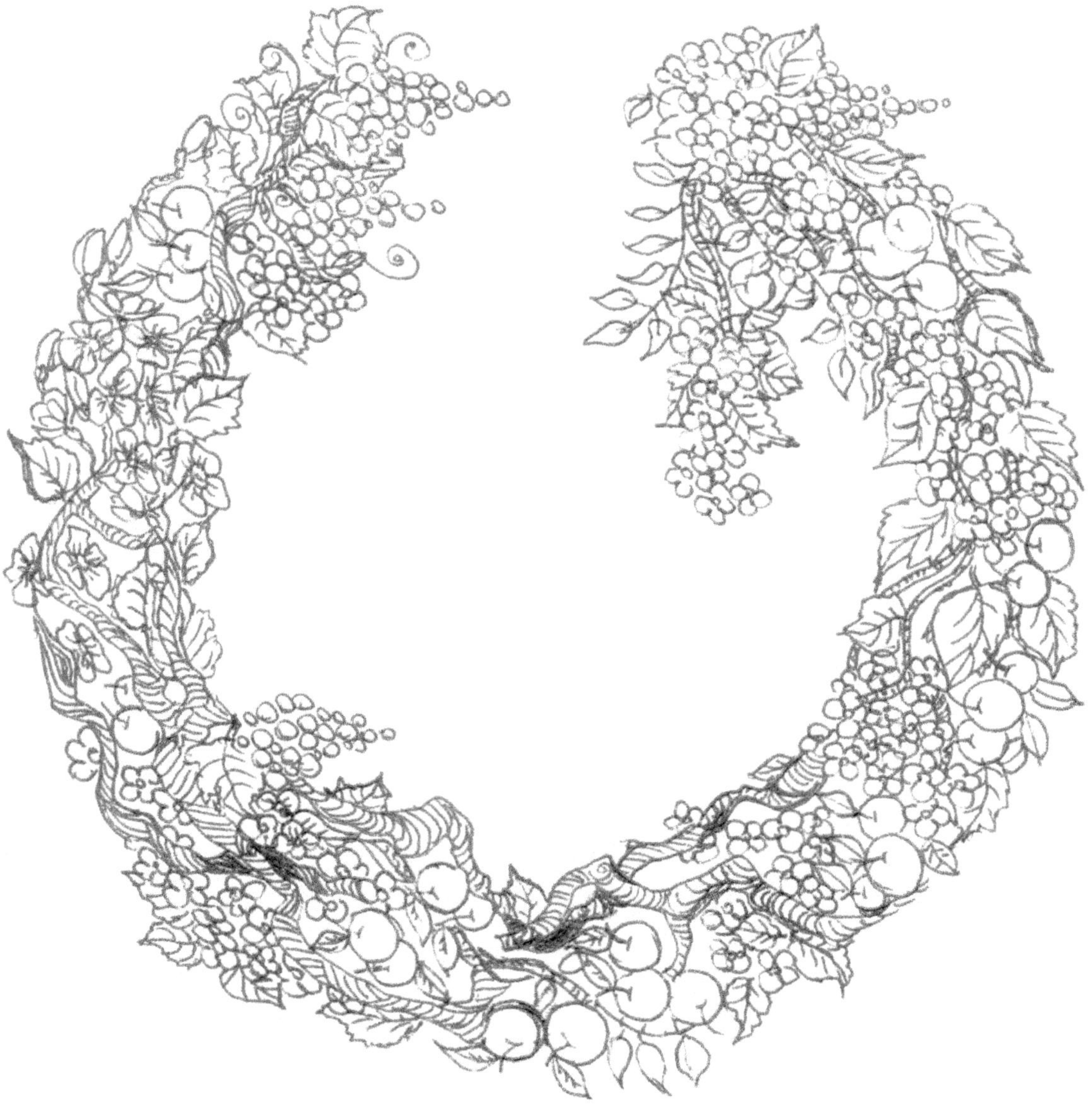

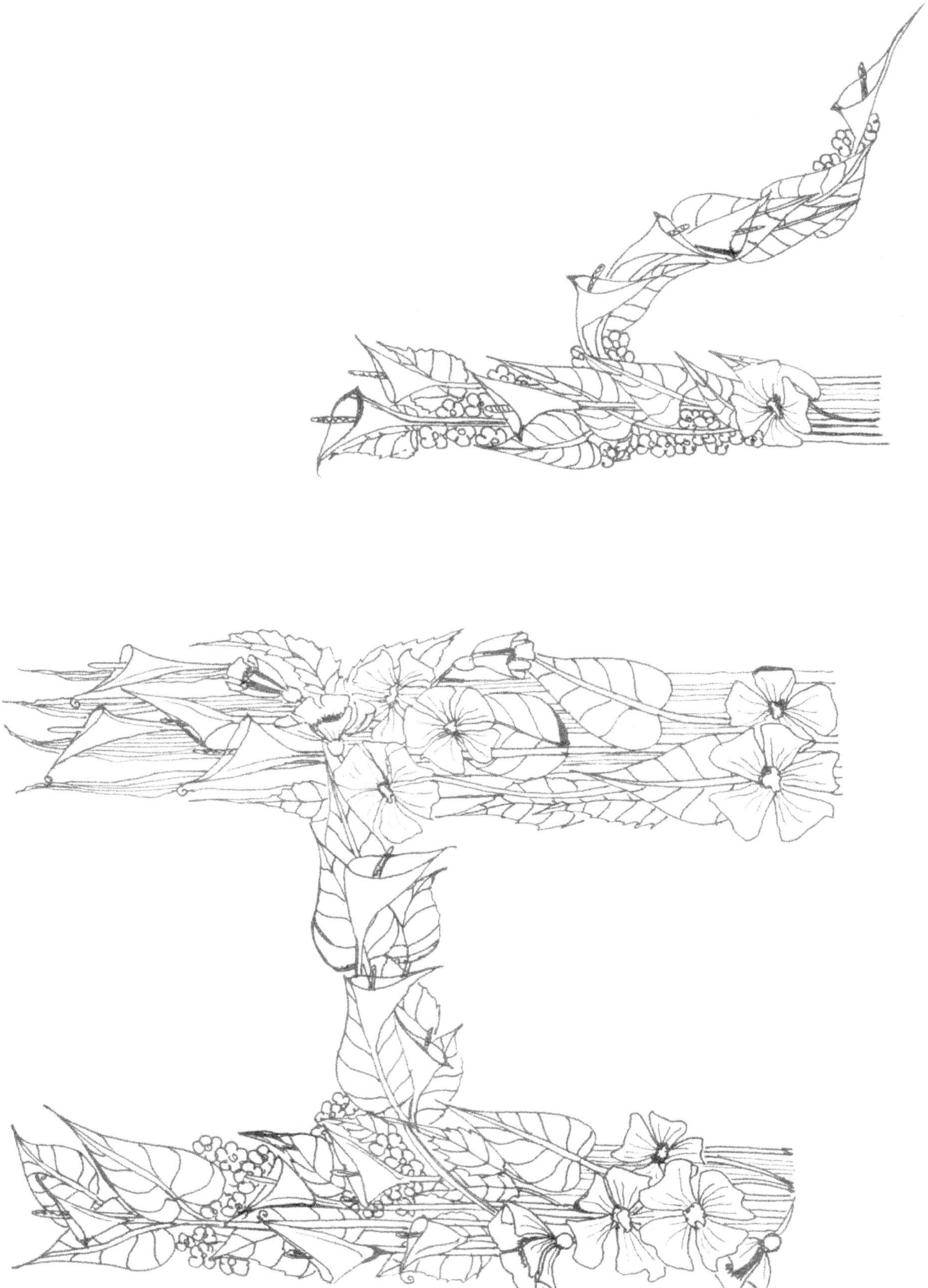

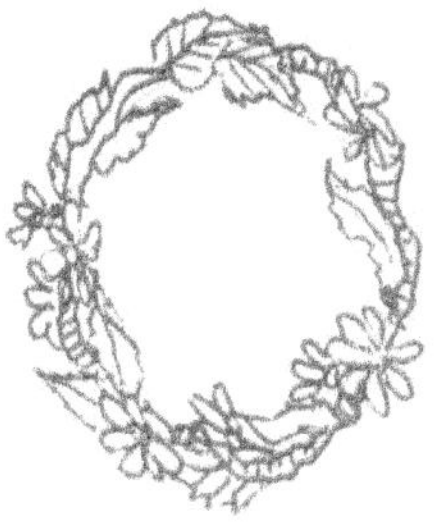

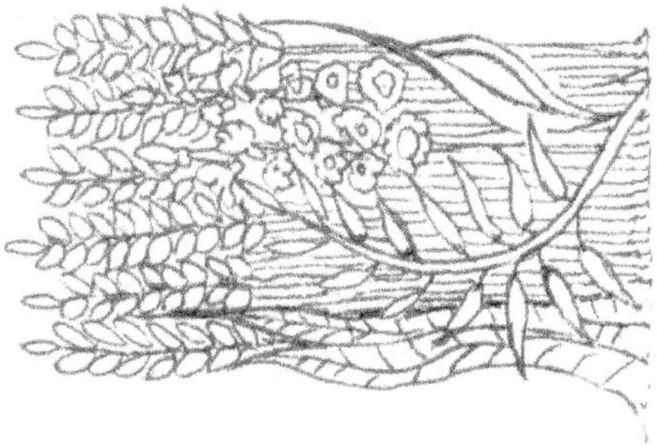

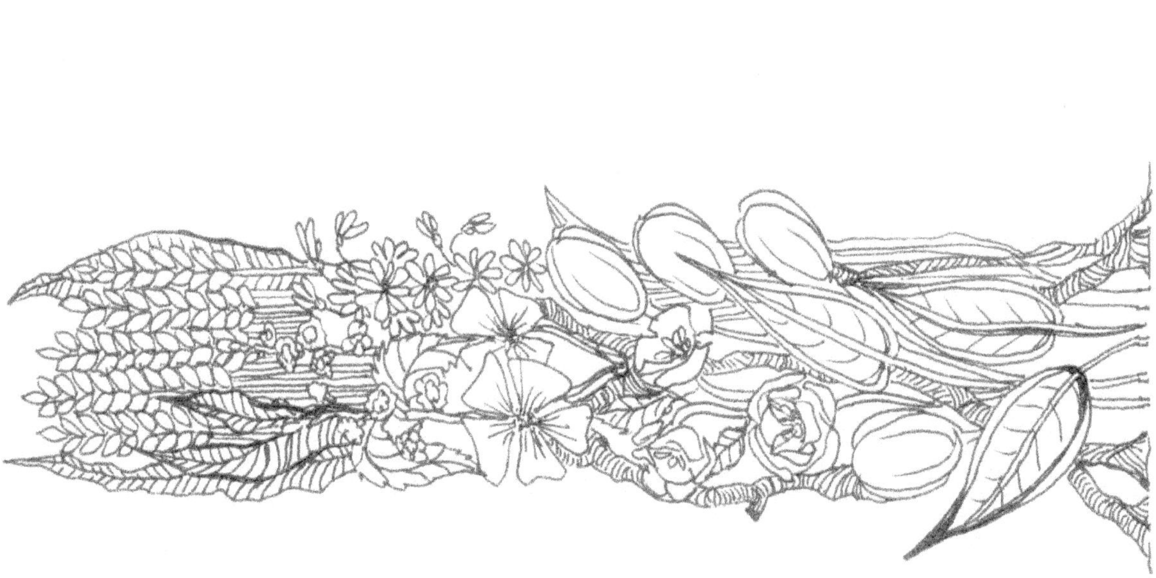

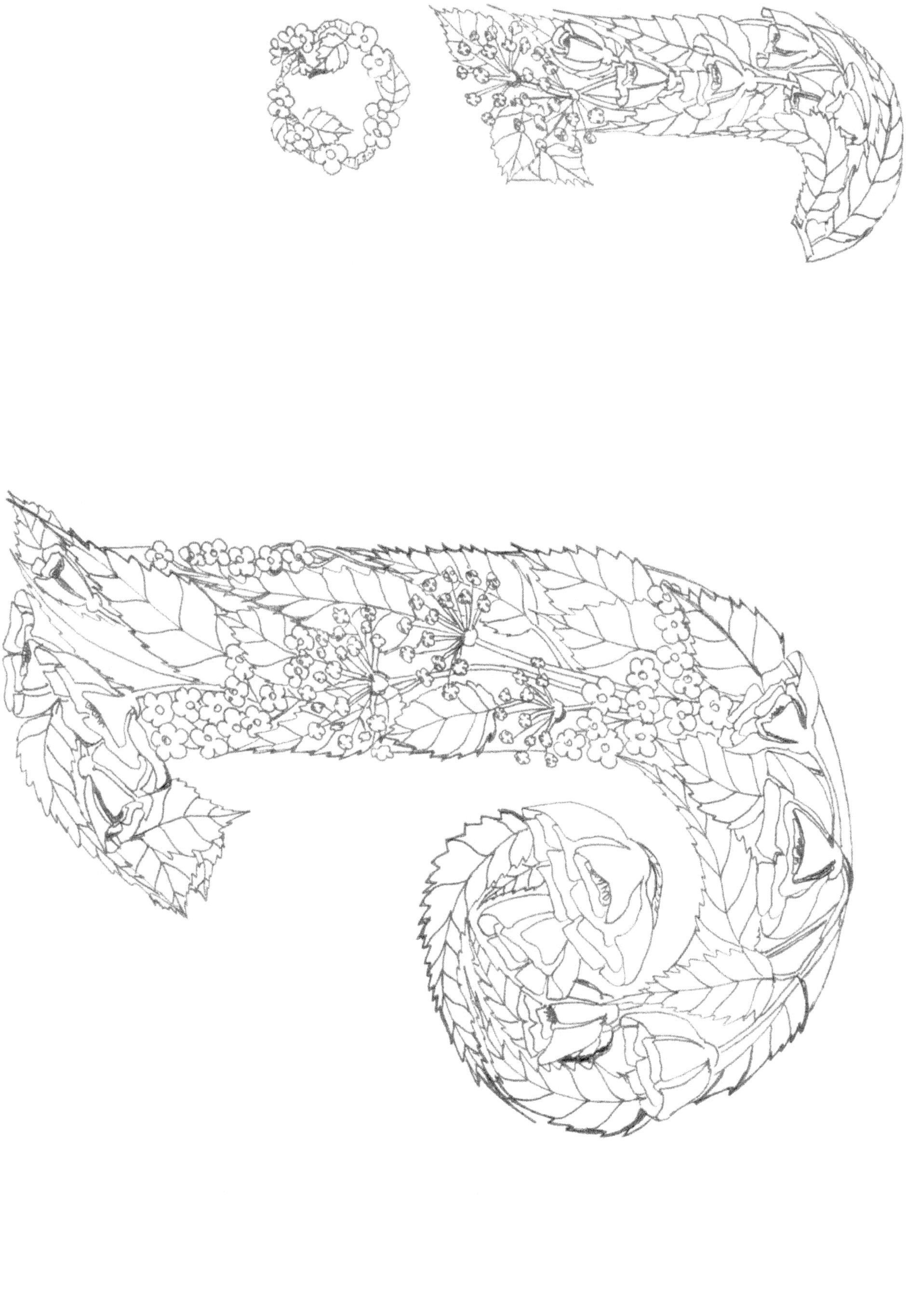

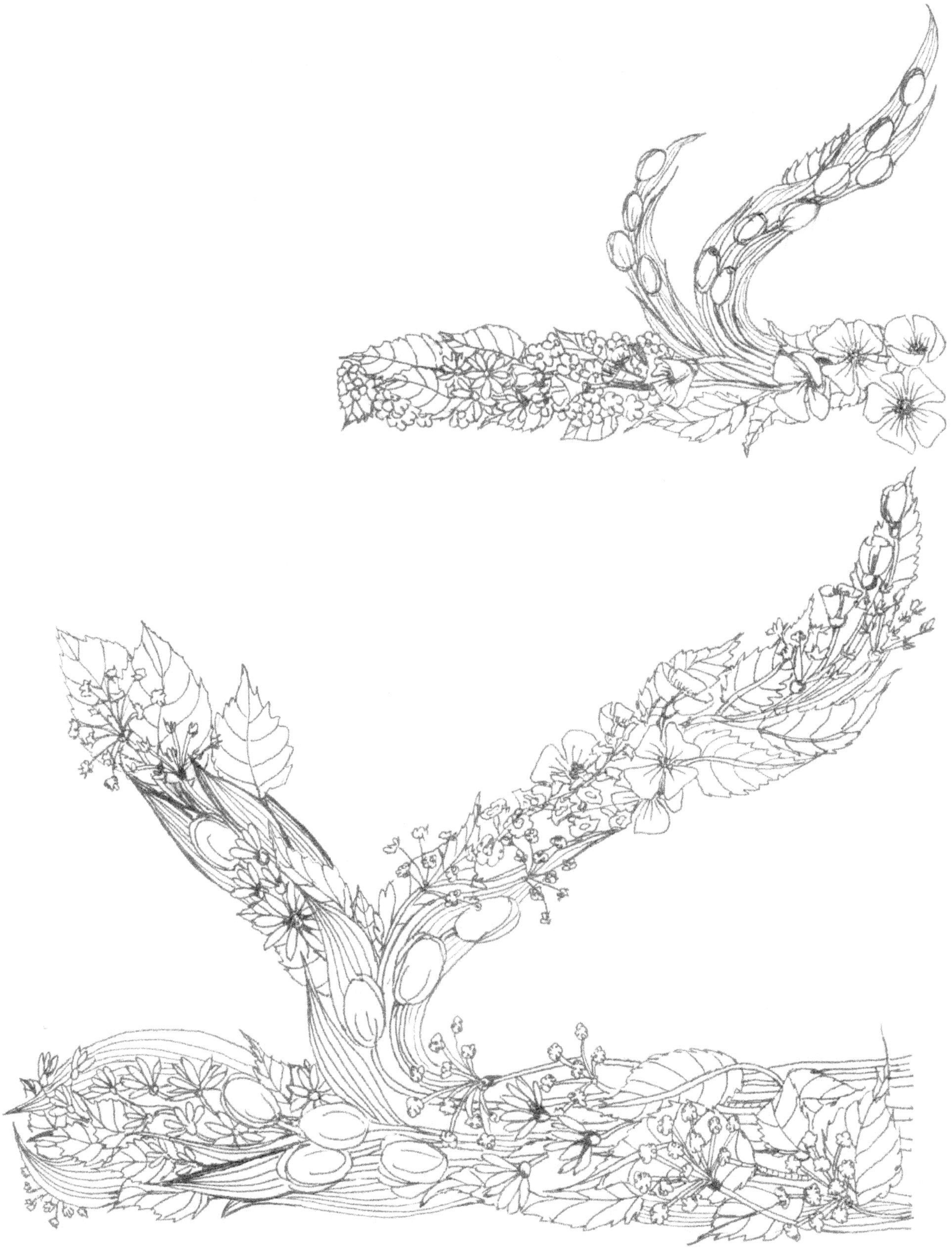

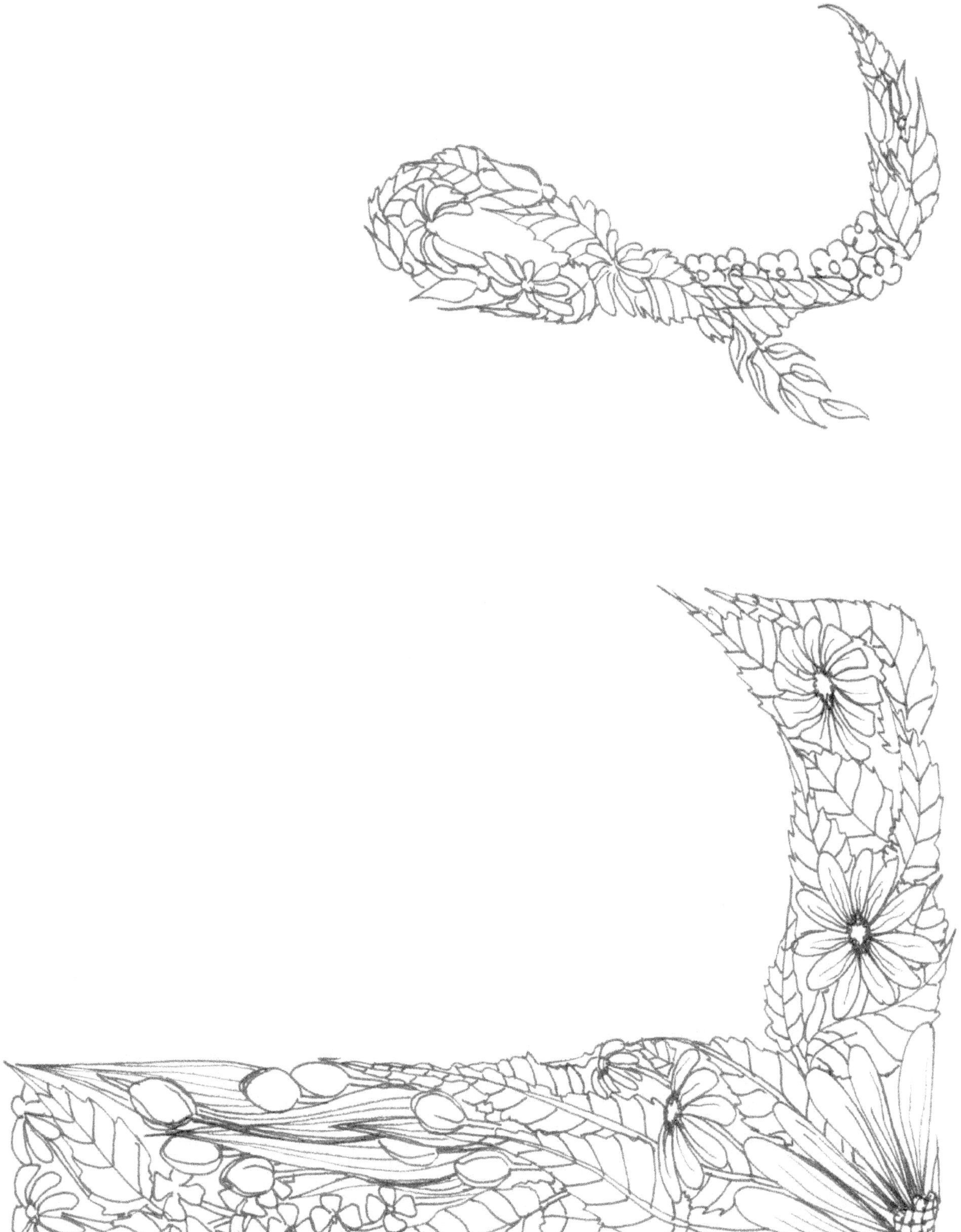

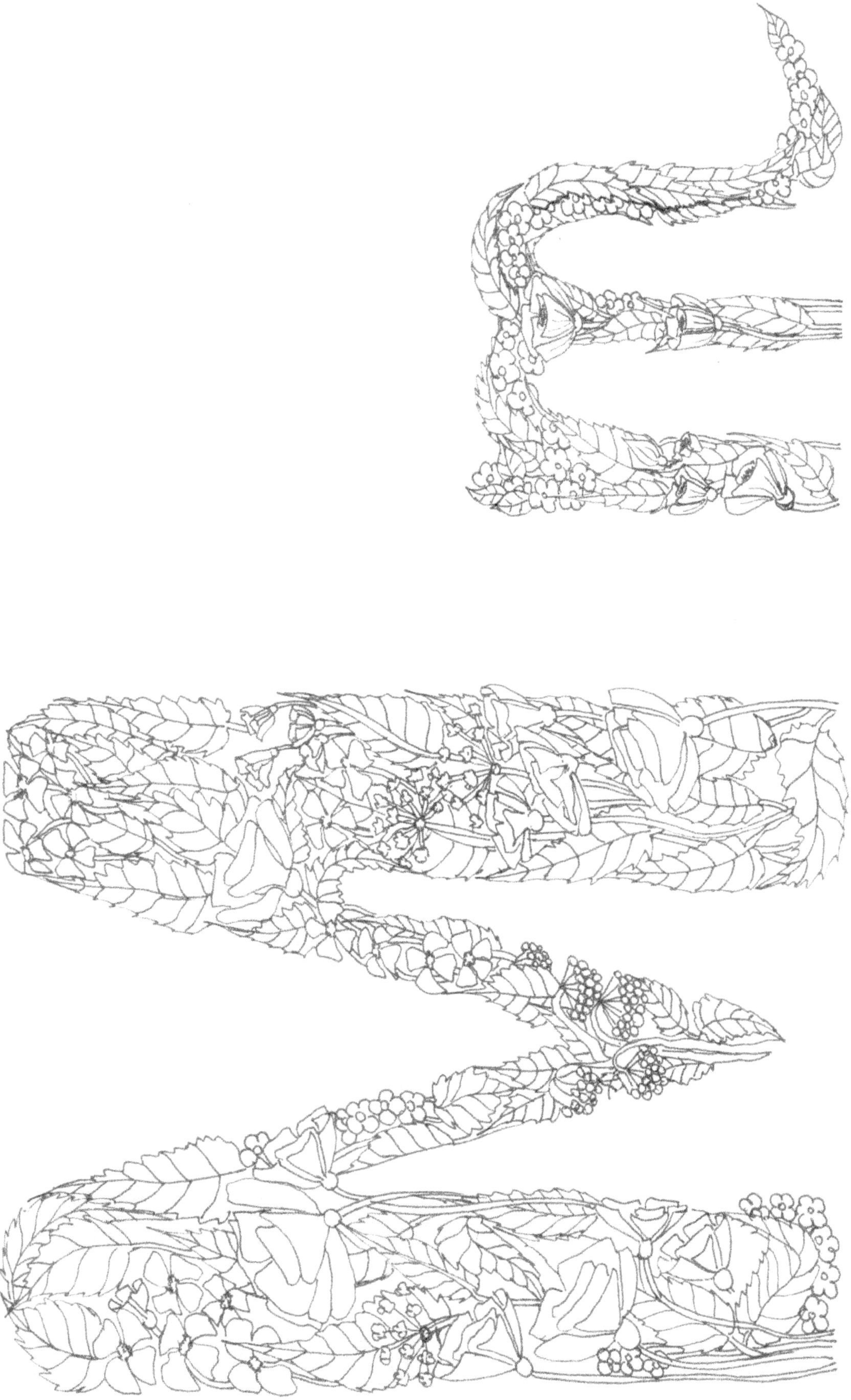

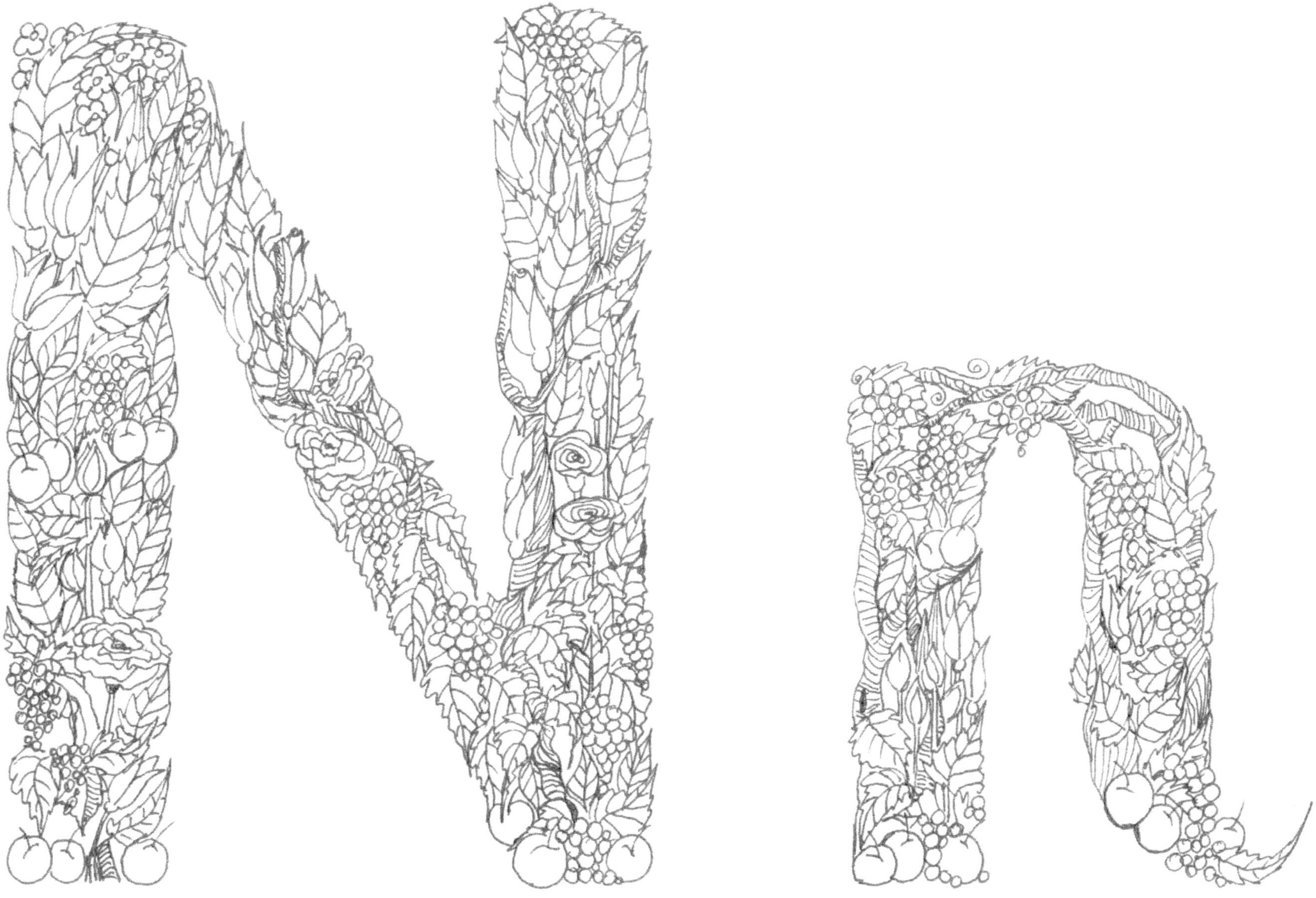
N n

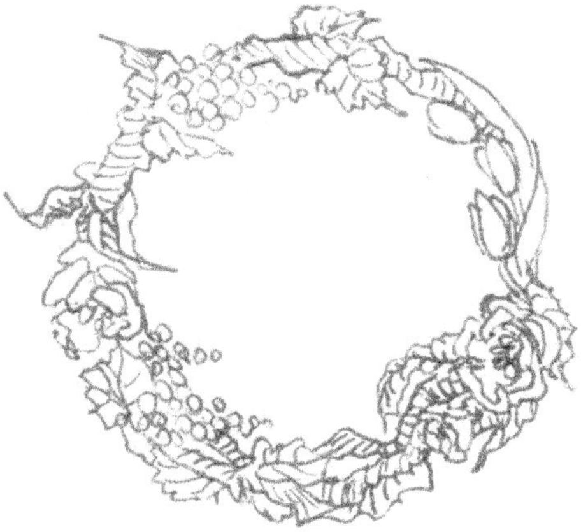

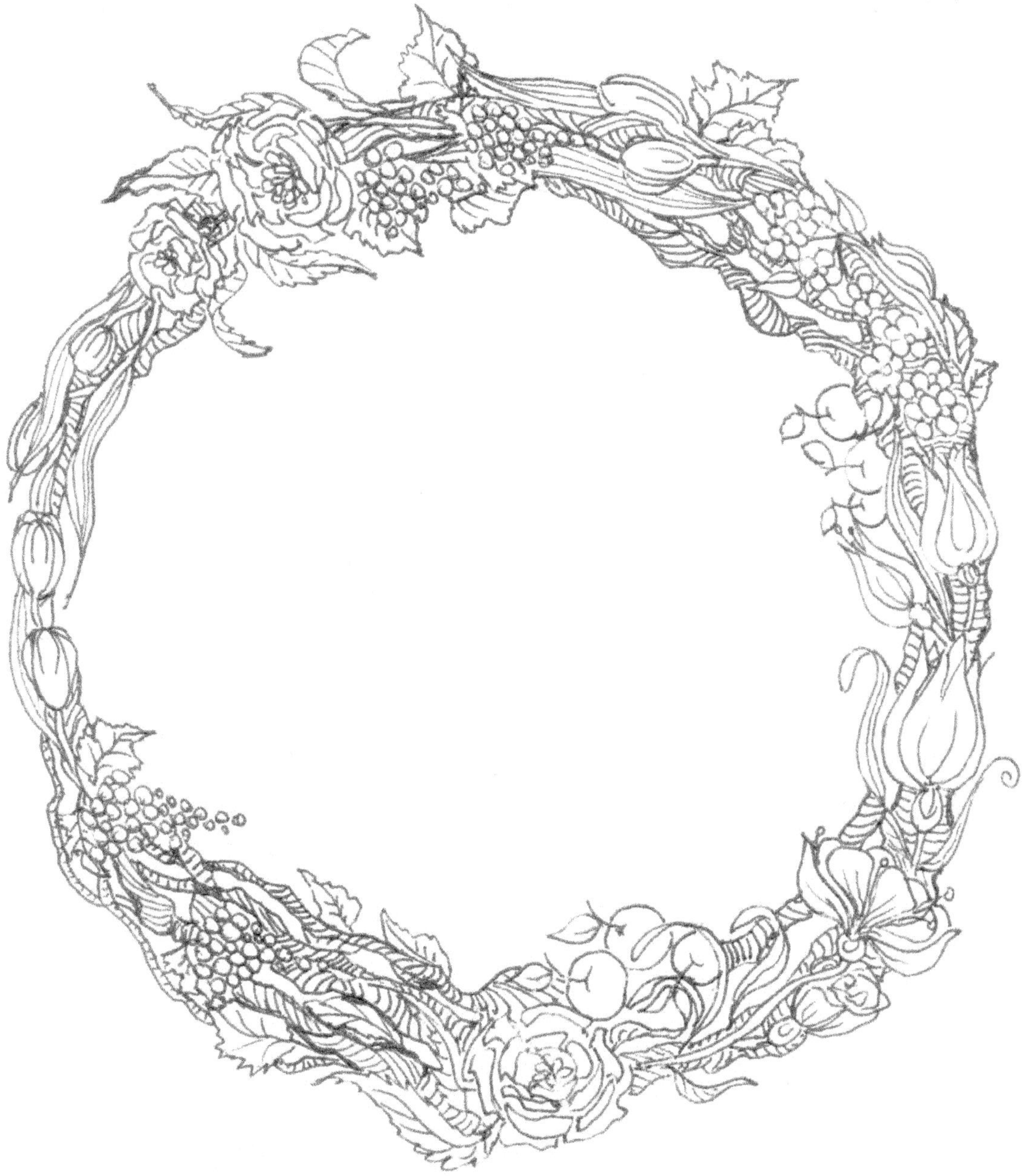

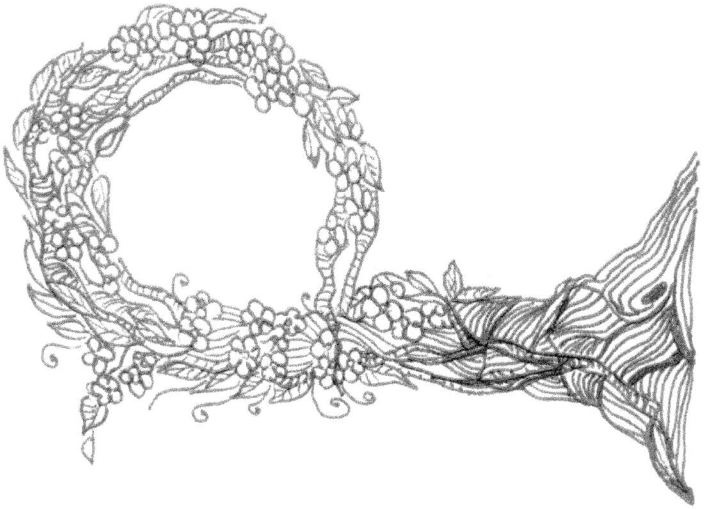

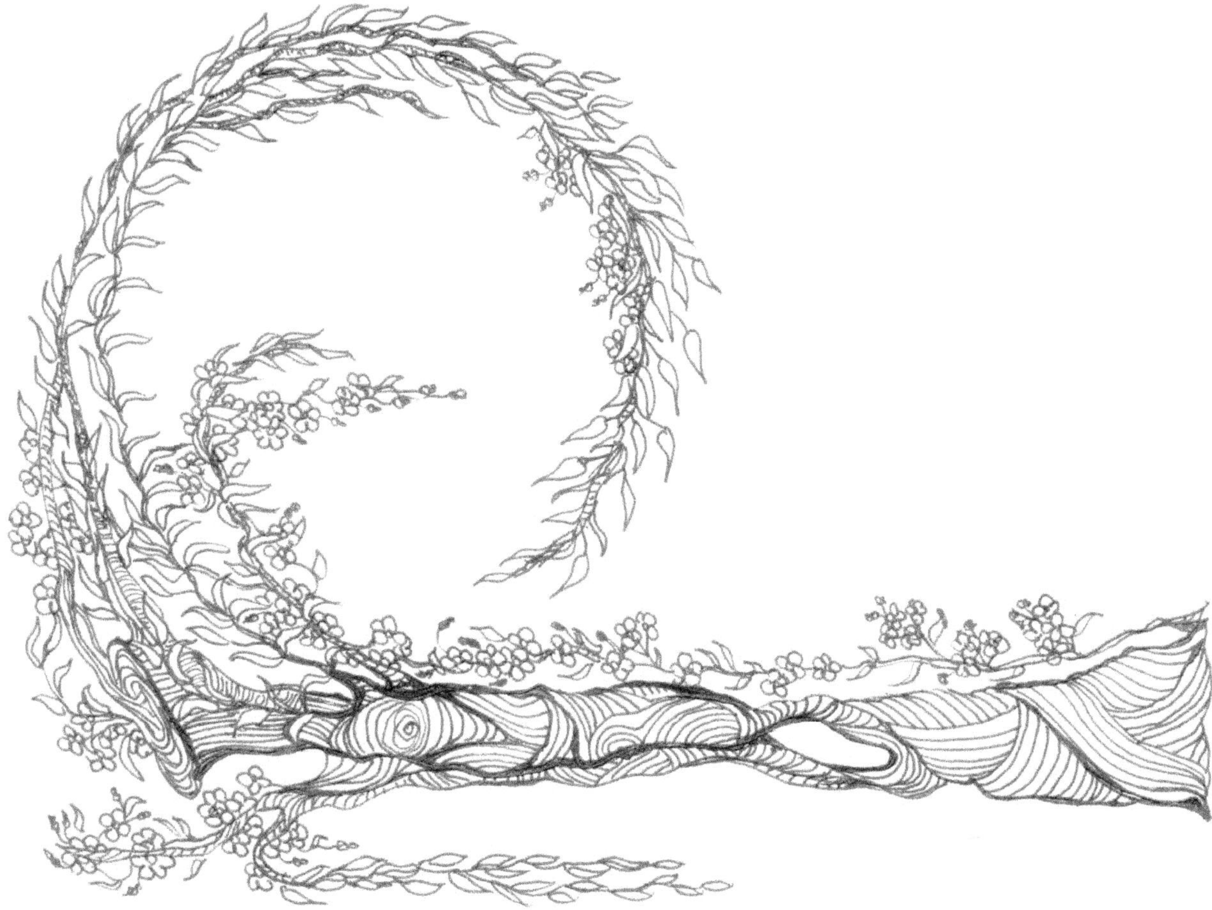

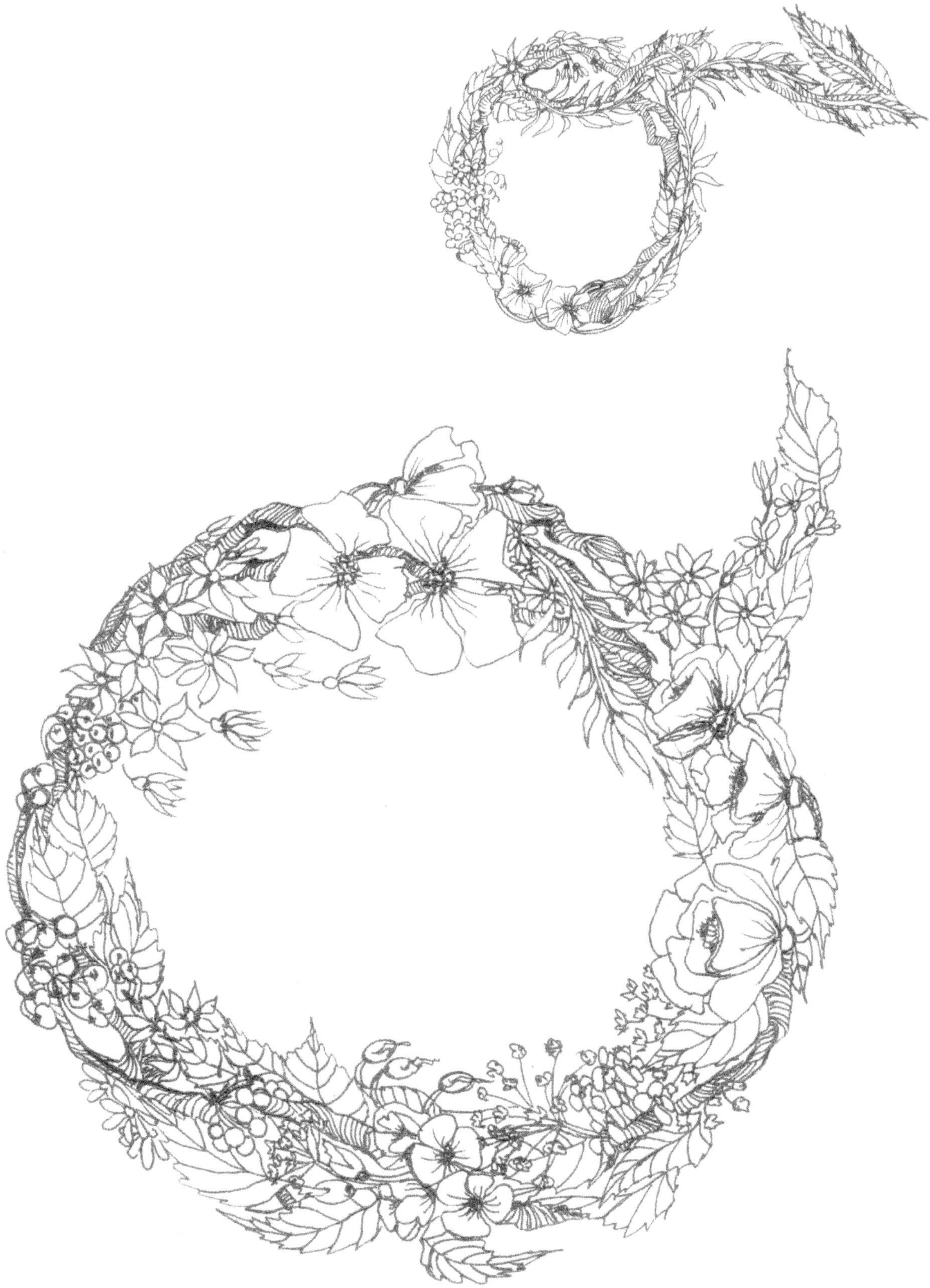

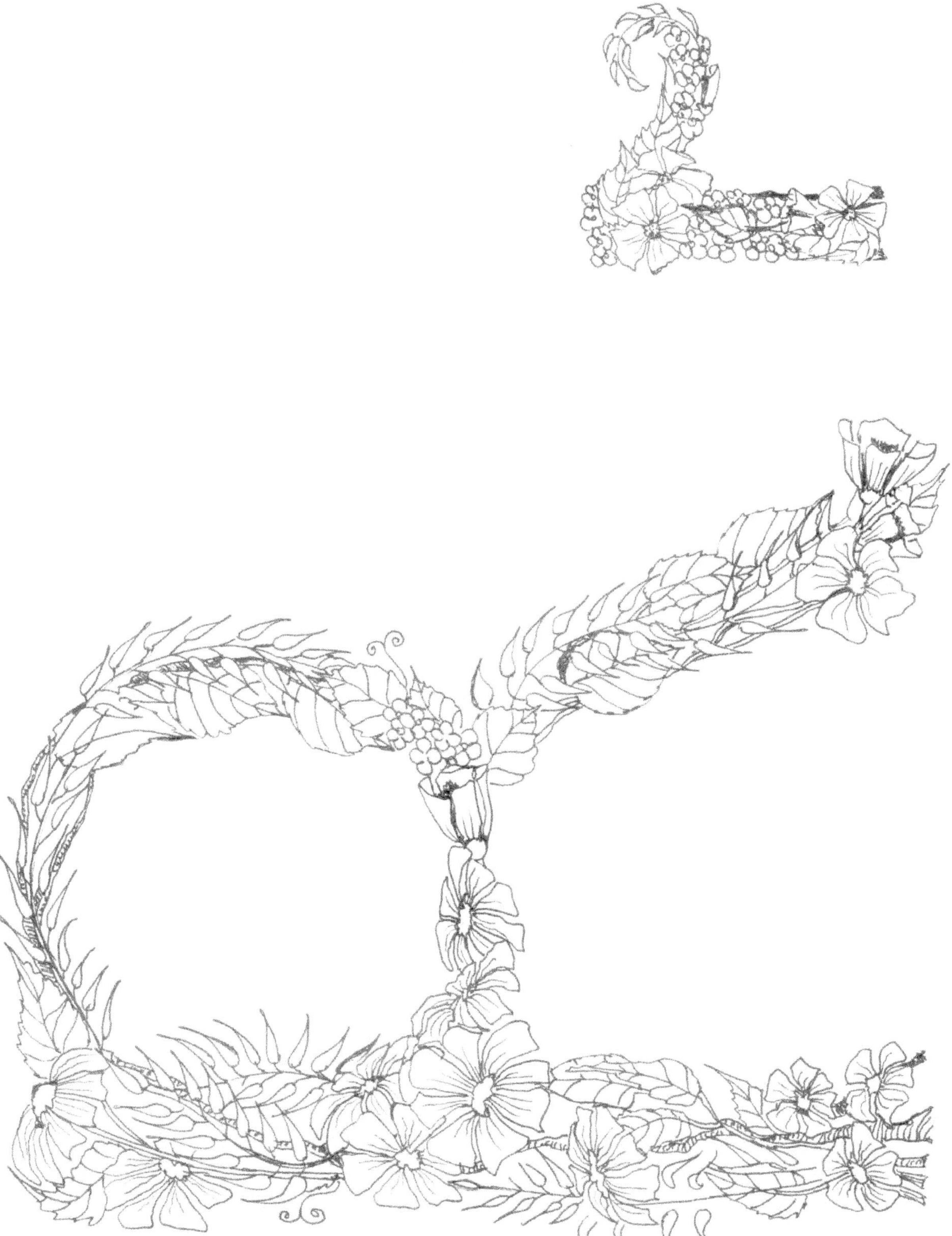

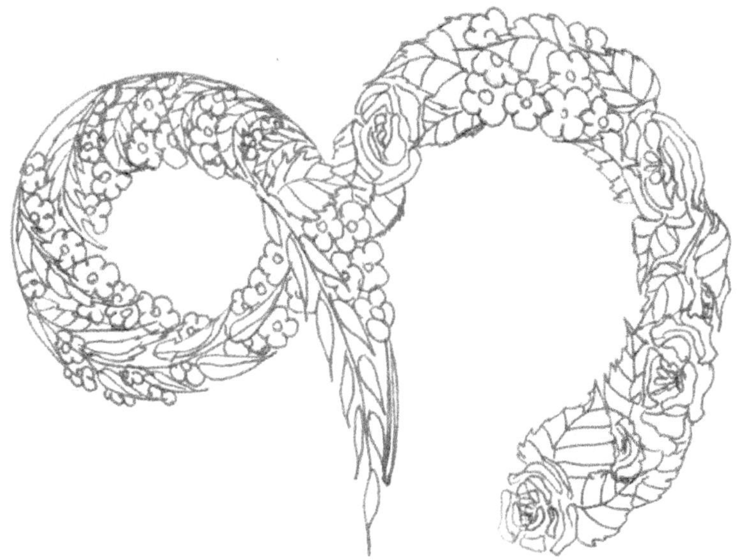

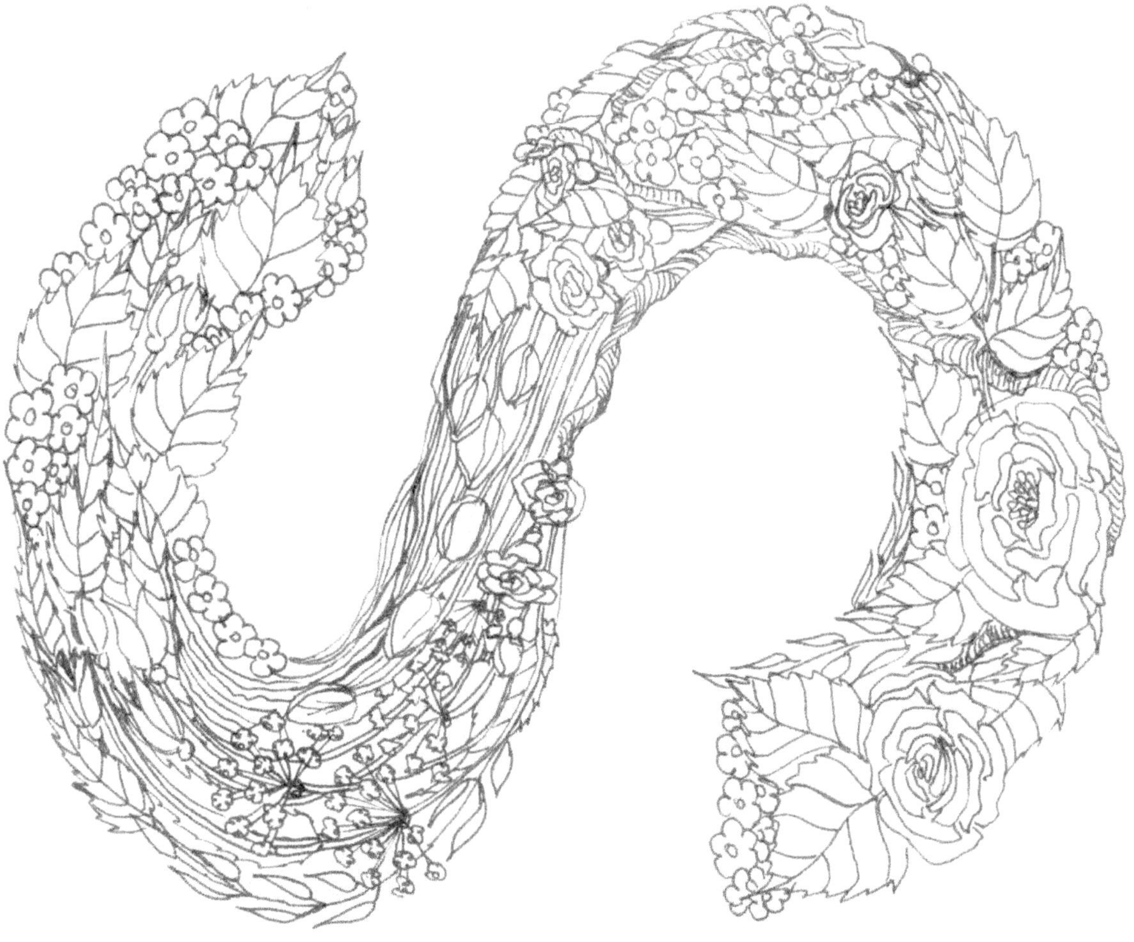

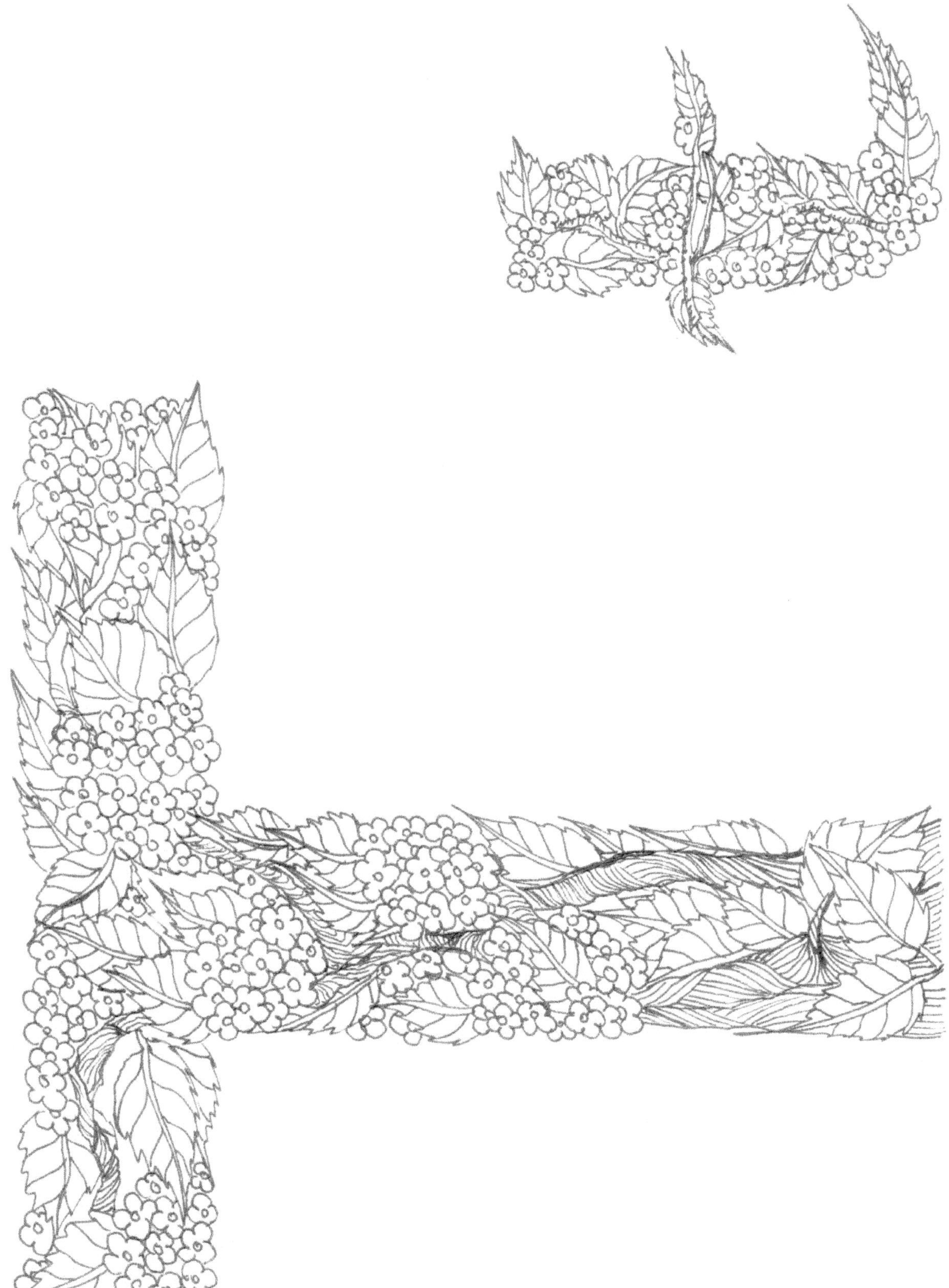

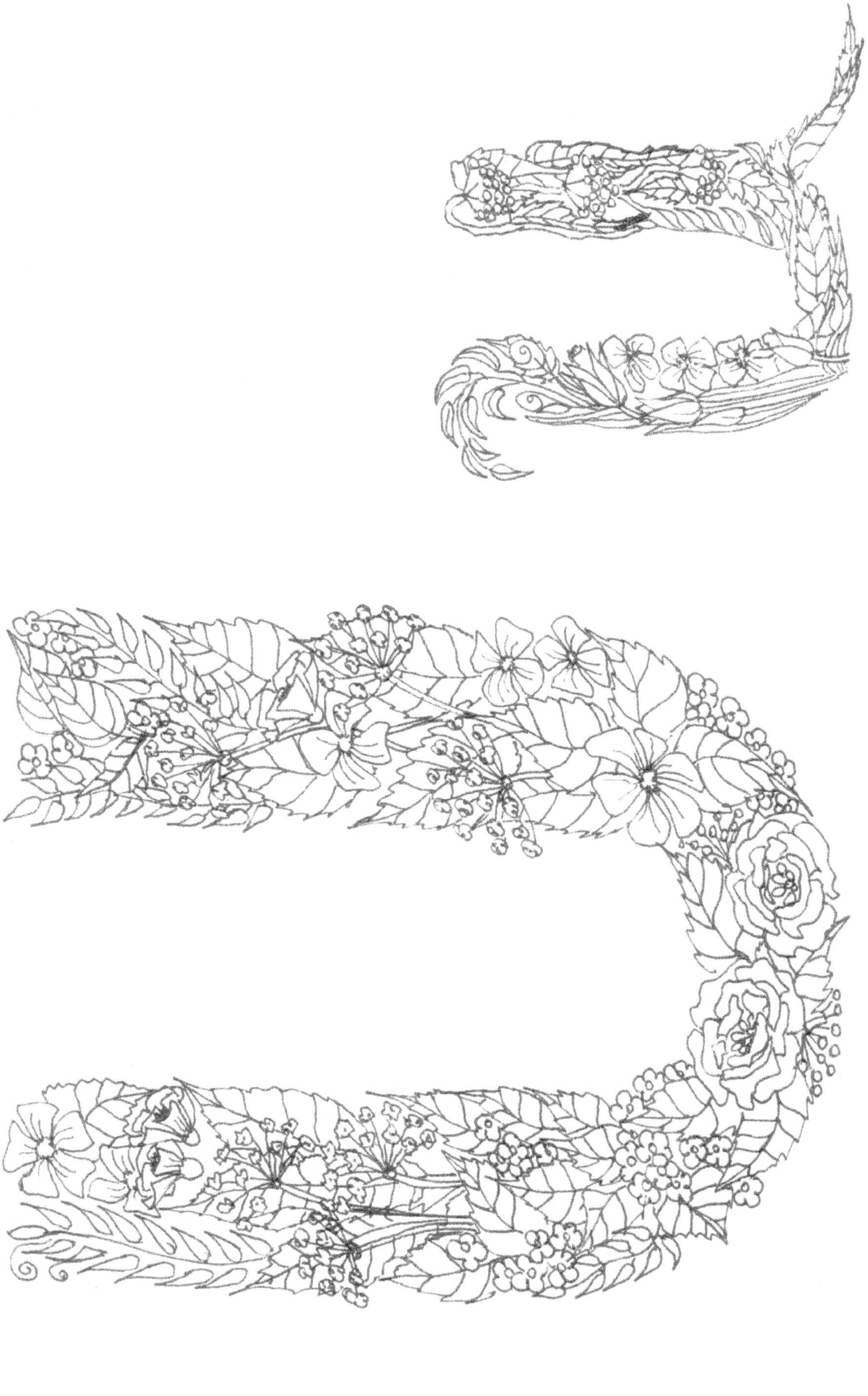

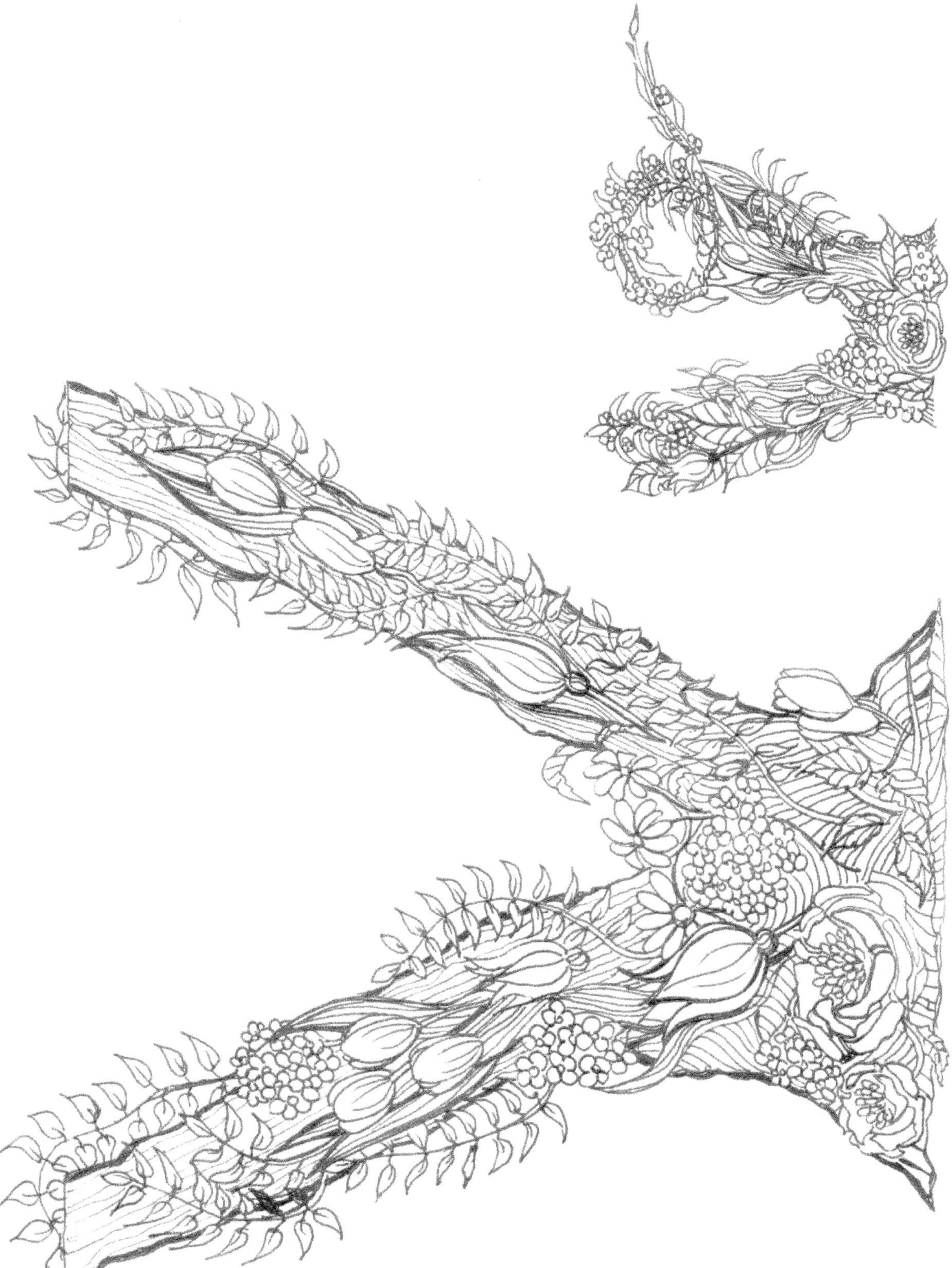

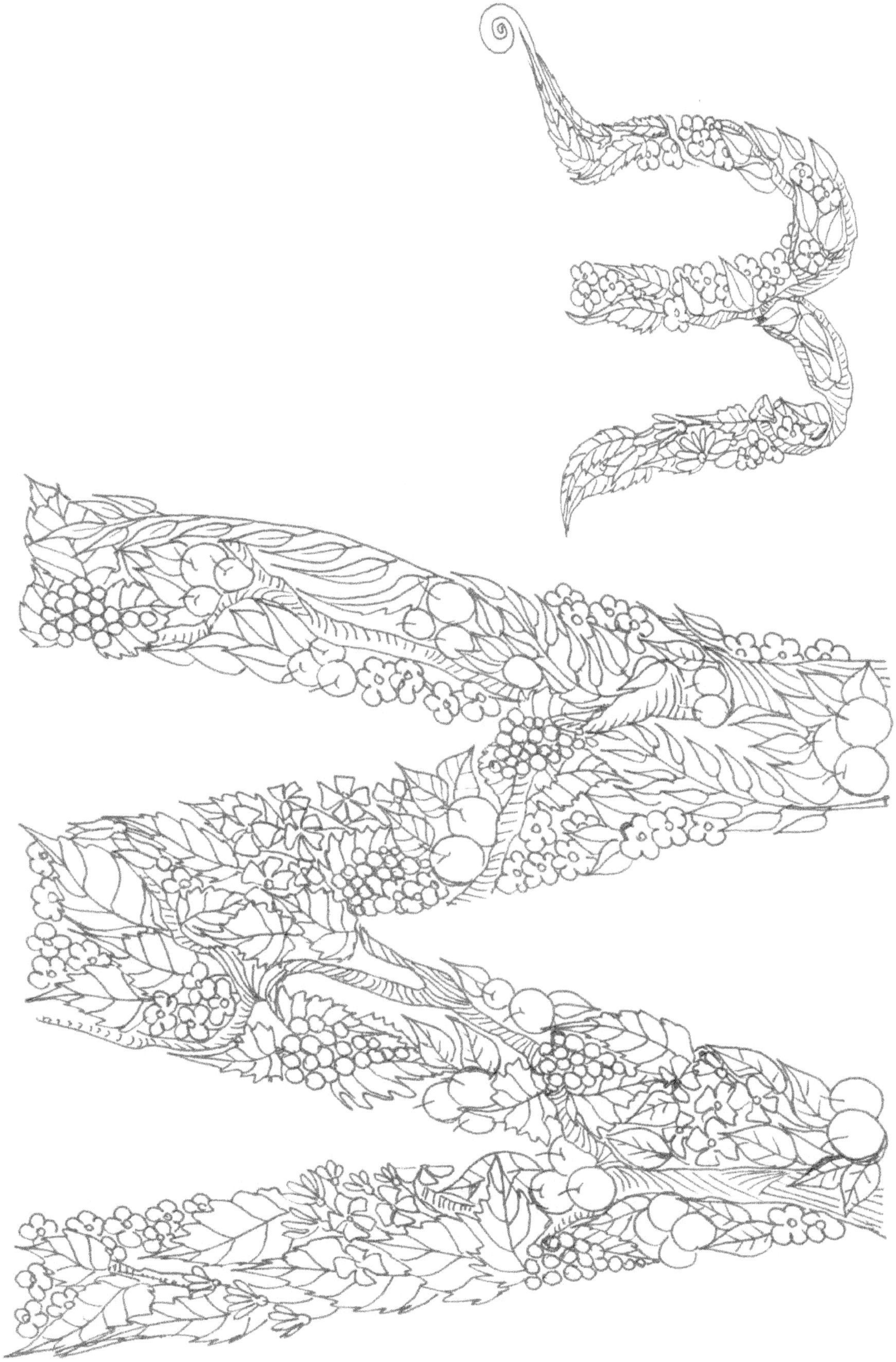

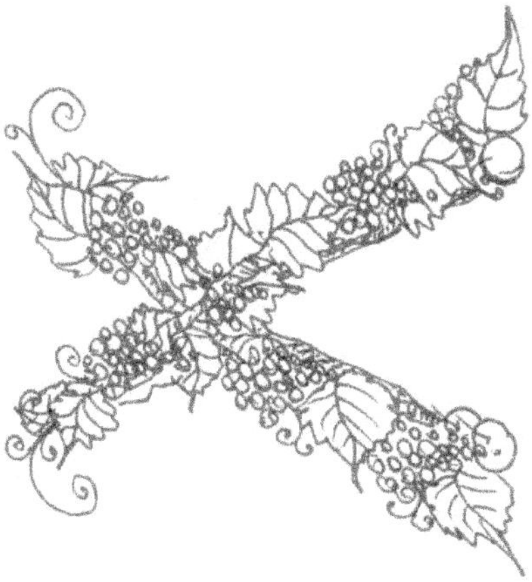

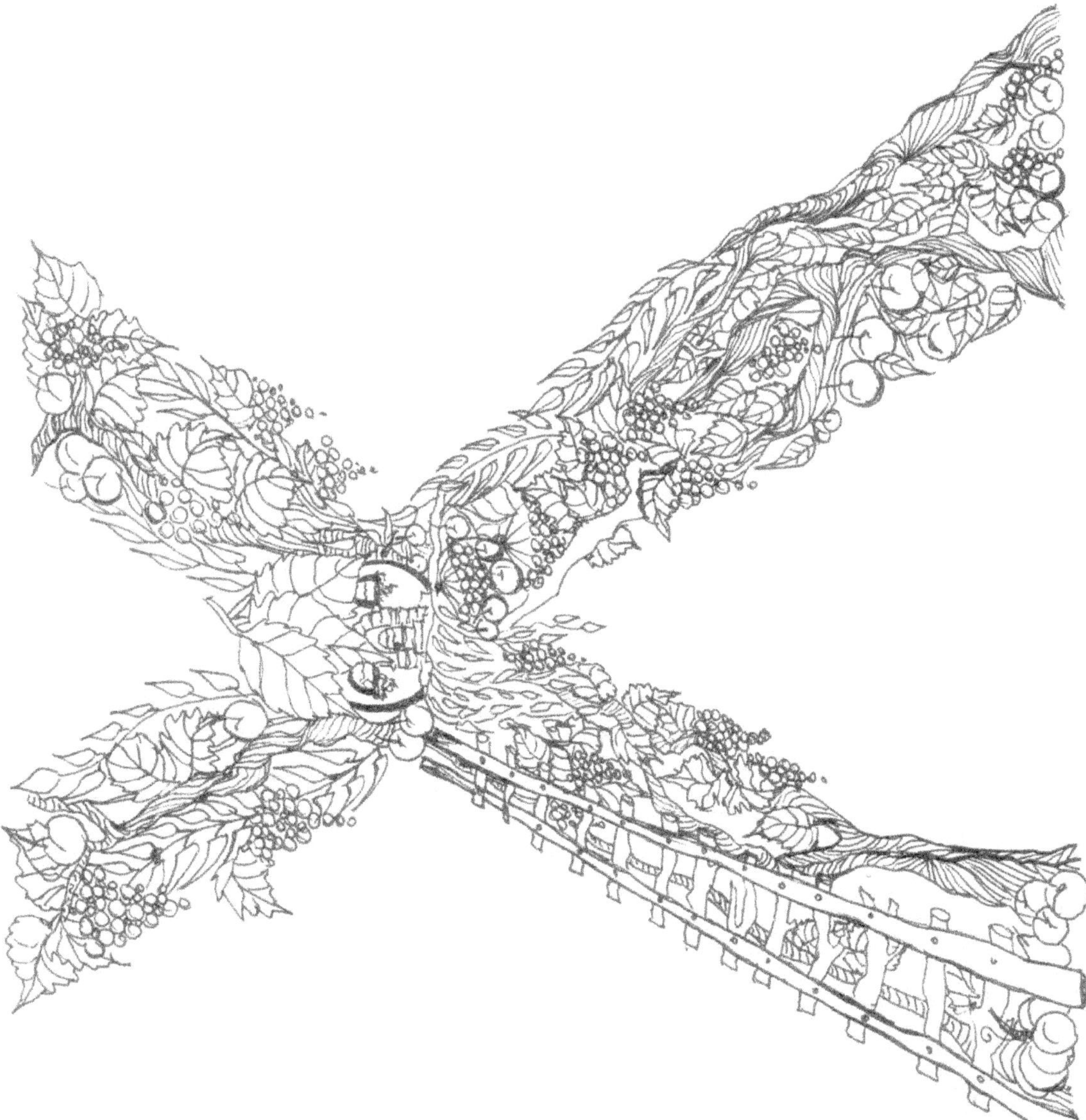

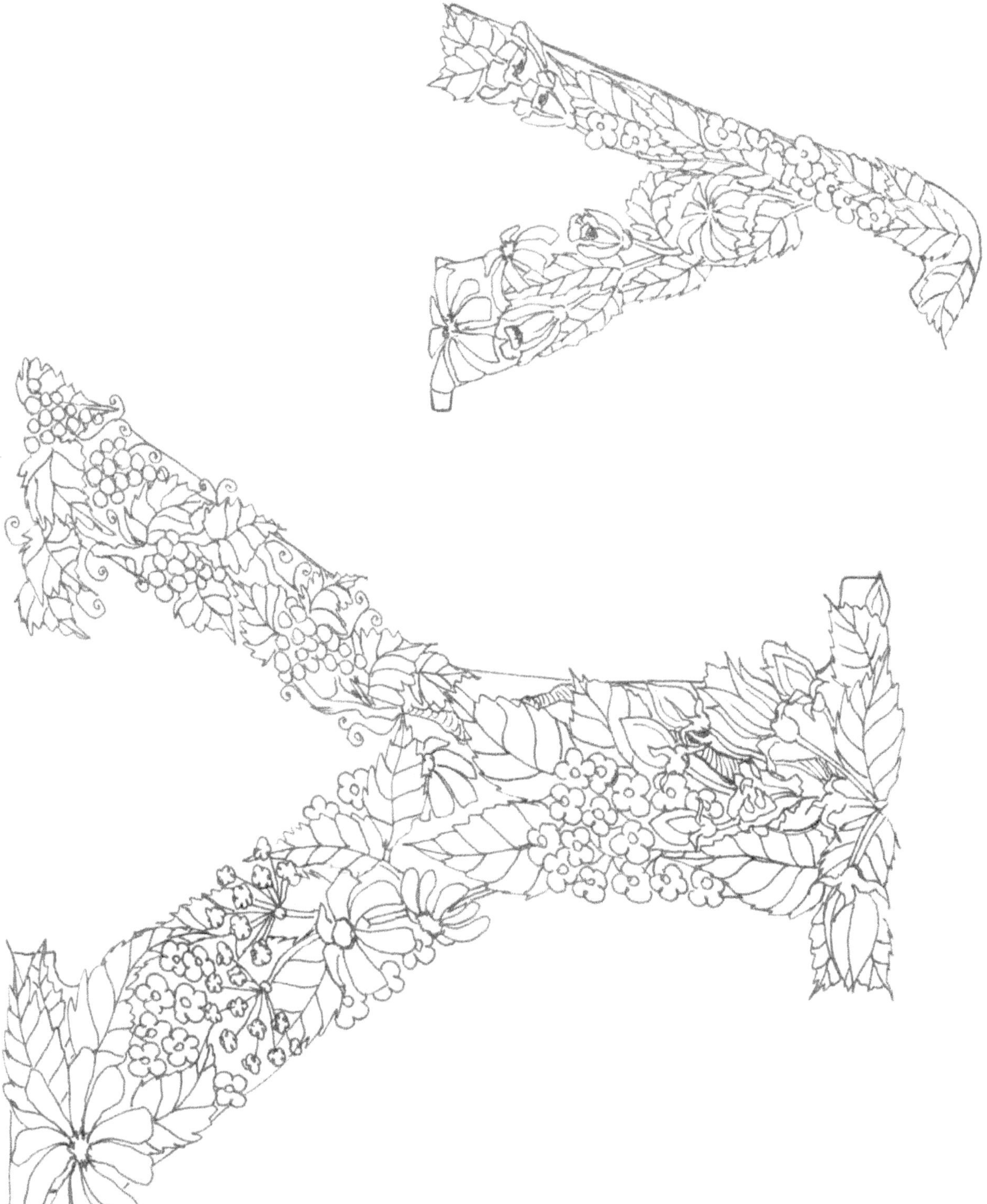

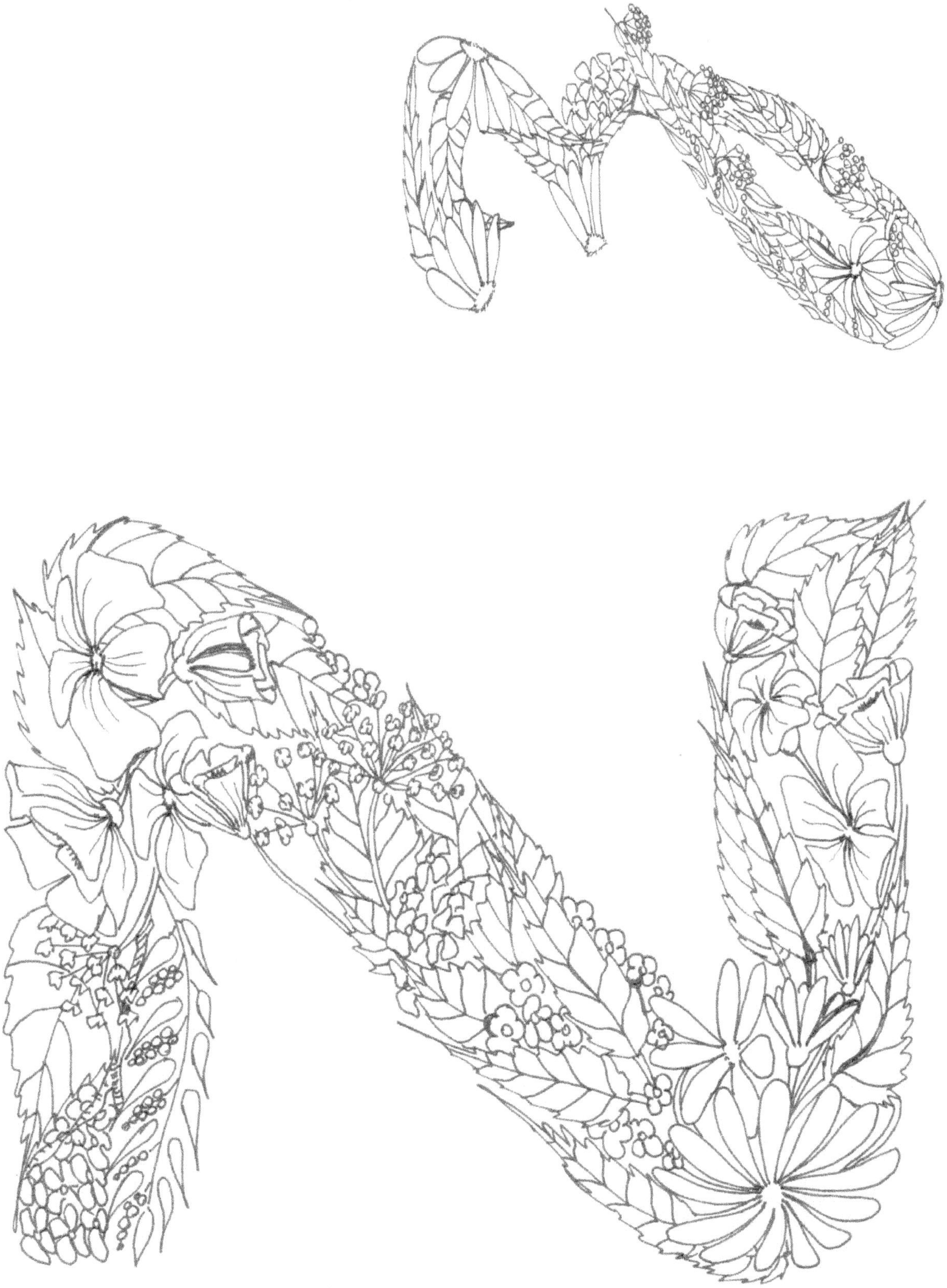

Everyone sees the world in one's own way

www.ingramcontent.com/pod-product-compliance
Lightning Source LLC
Chambersburg PA
CBHW081128180526
45170CB00008B/3043
* 9 7 8 1 5 4 0 4 3 7 0 7 5 *